THE SMARTEST ANIMALS

ELEPHANTS

by Tammy Gagne

Content Consultant
Raman Sukumar, PhD
Centre for Ecological Sciences
Indian Institute of Science

CORE
LIBRARY

Published by ABDO Publishing Company, PO Box 398166, Minneapolis, MN 55439. Copyright © 2014 by Abdo Consulting Group, Inc. International copyrights reserved in all countries. No part of this book may be reproduced in any form without written permission from the publisher. The Core Library™ is a trademark and logo of ABDO Publishing Company.

Printed in the United States of America,
North Mankato, Minnesota
092013
012014

Editor: Mirella Miller
Series Designer: Becky Daum

Library of Congress Cataloging-in-Publication Data
Gagne, Tammy.
  Elephants / by Tammy Gagne.
      pages cm. -- (The smartest animals)
  Includes bibliographical references and index.
  ISBN 978-1-62403-167-0
[1. Elephants--Juvenile literature.] I. Title.
  QL737.P98G34 2014
  599.67--dc23
                          2013027427

Photo Credits: Suranga Weeratunga/Shutterstock Images, cover, 1; iStockphoto/Thinkstock, 4, 11, 18, 20, 28, 45; Think Elephants International/AP Images, 6; Red Line Editorial, 9, 30; Galyna Andrushko/Shutterstock Images, 12, 43; Anup Shah/Digital Vision/Thinkstock, 15; Schalk van Zuydam/AP Images, 17; Stephen Mudiari/Africa Media Online/AP Images, 23; Fuse/Thinkstock, 25; imagebroker.net/SuperStock, 26; Anupam Nath/AP Images, 31; Jason Straziuso/AP Images, 33; Rex Features/AP Images, 36; Eranga Jayawardena/AP Images, 39

CONTENTS

CHAPTER ONE

HEAD OF THE CLASS

The test course looked like a challenge from a reality television show. The test took place in Lampang, Thailand. Researchers from the Thai Elephant Conservation Center filled two red bowls with corn. They set the bowls on a table with wheels near the two elephants. A volleyball net stood between the elephants and the bowls of corn. Each elephant had a rope. It could use the rope to pull

Elephants are super-smart animals found in Africa and Asia.

Two elephants pull a table carrying a food reward.

the table under the net. But the rope would release
if only one elephant tugged on it. The elephants
had to work together to get the reward. Or so the
researchers thought.

The test was created to see if the elephants
could figure out they had to pull on the ropes at the

same time. Twelve elephants took part. Most of the elephants got the corn. One elephant did more than pass the test, though. The youngest elephant, Neua Un, found a way to cheat. Neua Un quickly realized she could get the reward without doing any work. She held her rope down with her foot while her partner did all the pulling.

The elephants had outsmarted the Thai researchers. But the researchers were still happy. Scientists consider elephants to be among the smartest animals. But intelligence tests for elephants are rare. This is because elephants' size makes it difficult and sometimes unsafe to work with them.

Enormous Elephants

Elephants are enormous. There are two types of elephants—African elephants and Asian elephants. Of all the land animals in the world, African elephants are the largest. Male African elephants stand between 9 feet and 12 feet (2.7 m and 3.6 m) tall at their shoulders. They weigh up to 15,000 pounds (6,803 kg). Asian elephants are smaller than African elephants. Males are between 8 feet and 10.5 feet (2.4 m and 3 m) tall. They weigh up to 12,000 pounds (5,500 kg). Female African and Asian elephants are smaller than males. However, females still weigh nearly as much as males.

Special Body Parts

Elephants' long noses, or trunks, make them special animals. The trunk is an extension of the upper lip. It serves as an extra limb. The trunk contains approximately 100,000 muscles and tendons that help it move. It has small

African or Asian?

Size is not the only difference between African and Asian elephants. Asian elephants have smaller, triangular ears. African elephants have larger, rounded ears. All African elephants have tusks. Only some male Asian elephants have tusks. Asian elephants' tusks are smaller than African elephants' tusks. African elephants have two small fingers at the bottom of the trunk. Asian elephants have one finger.

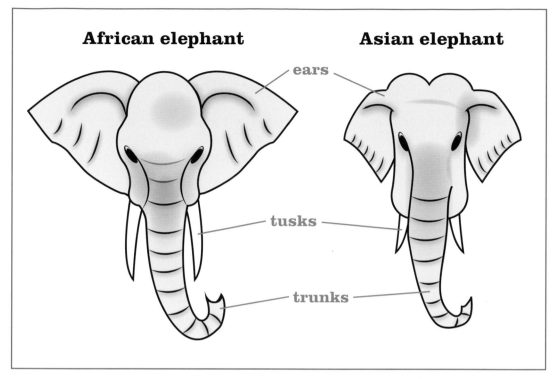

African elephant   **Asian elephant**

ears

tusks

trunks

A Head Start to Telling Them Apart

This diagram shows an African elephant's head and an Asian elephant's head. After reading about the two elephants, what did you imagine they looked like? How does seeing them next to each other help you better understand their differences?

fingers at the bottom for grasping objects. Elephants use their trunks for breathing and smelling. They also use them for drinking and feeding themselves. Elephants even use their trunks for self-defense.

Another body part that makes an elephant special is its tusks. Most full-grown tusks weigh

9

In with the New

Elephants have six sets of molars that can come in during their lifetimes. As an elephant grinds a tooth down from eating, a new one grows in. The old tooth is replaced from behind. Sometimes parts of two teeth are present at one time. Each set of teeth will last a bit longer than the set before it did. An elephant usually has its final set of teeth when it is between 25 and 45 years old.

between 100 pounds and 175 pounds (45 kg and 79 kg) each!

An elephant's body is covered with thick, gray skin. The skin can be as deep as 1.5 inches (3.8 cm). Elephants have wrinkles all over their bodies that keep them cool. Water trapped between these wrinkles takes a while to evaporate.

Elephant tusks are teeth that extend from the tops of their mouths.

CHAPTER TWO

LIFE IN THE HERD

Elephants live in close family groups of females. Multiple family groups gather together to create a herd. Between 8 and 100 elephants live in a herd. The size of a herd depends on the surroundings and family sizes. Scientists believe the leader of a herd is its oldest and largest female. She is called the matriarch. The matriarch leads the herd until her death. Her oldest daughter then becomes matriarch.

Elephant herds are made up of family groups.

Leading the Way

The matriarch of a herd is not a ruler. Unless the herd is facing immediate danger, all of the adult females in the herd make decisions together. If they are in danger, though, they turn to the matriarch for guidance. It is easy to spot the herds with the oldest matriarchs. These groups tend to survive the best under the worst conditions. They often have the most calves.

Males leave the herd between the ages of 12 and 15 years old. They live alone or with other male elephants. An adult male interacts with a herd when he is looking for a mate.

Mating

Females start mating between the ages of 12 and 14 years old. Most females give birth to one calf at a time. There have been very few cases of twin calves being born. Females give birth every three to six years. Females may continue to give birth until they are 60 years old. They will mate with multiple males throughout their lifetimes. Males do not help raise their calves.

Elephant calves are well cared for by their mothers and other females in the herd.

Female elephants are pregnant for approximately 22 months. Shortly after a calf is born, it can stand by itself. The calf starts walking approximately one to two hours later. Newborn calves measure approximately

Holy Cow!

As soon as a calf is born, it begins nursing. It can drink up to 20 pints (9.5 L) of its mother's milk each day during its first four months. The milk contains large amounts of fat and protein. All this nutrition helps the calf gain approximately 30 pounds (14 kg) a week!

3 feet (1 m) tall and weigh approximately 200 pounds (91 kg).

Raised by a Herd

A calf is raised and protected by the whole herd. Aunts, sisters, and cousins help care for the youngest members of the herd. These babysitters are called *allomothers*. Calves depend on their mothers and allomothers for five years.

When a calf is born, the herd changes its daily routine to suit the needs of the new baby. Adults slow down their pace so the calf can keep up. They show the young elephant which plants are safe to eat and how to eat them. As young elephants grow, they learn to become independent by watching and copying other elephants. When the calf is four months old, it starts to practice using its trunk to grab things.

An elephant herd is responsible for helping a mother care for a young elephant.

Life Expectancy

Elephants can live up to 70 years depending on their surroundings. Scientists have found that many elephants living in the wild live almost twice as long

It is important for elephants to live with their mothers and relatives for the first few years of their lives.

as elephants born in zoos. Calves face a higher risk of death when born in zoos than when born in the wild. Zoologists believe this is because the calves are often taken away from their mothers and other relatives. Calves in the wild stay close to their mothers.

G. A. Bradshaw is an animal psychologist. In her book, *Elephants on the Edge*, she writes about elephant research in Africa and what makes these animals so special:

Elephants' personalities are as diverse as those of humans. A pilot study investigating elephant personalities . . . found that a group of eleven female elephants "show consistent differences between individuals in . . . personality traits" . . . . [elephants] can be happy or sad, volatile or placid. They display envy, jealousy, throw tantrums and are fiercely competitive . . . They grieve deeply for lost loved ones. . . . They have a sense of compassion that projects beyond their own kind and sometimes extends to others in distress. They help one another . . . miss an absent loved one, and when you know them really well, you can see that they even smile when having fun and are happy.

Source: G. A. Bradshaw. Elephants on the Edge: What Animals Teach Us About Humanity. *New Haven, CT: Yale University Press, 2009. Print. 24.*

What's the Big Idea?

Take a close look at Bradshaw's words. What is her main idea? What evidence is used to support her point? Come up with a few sentences showing how Bradshaw uses two or three pieces of evidence to support her main point.

CHAPTER THREE

USING THEIR HEADS

Elephants are ranked as one of the most intelligent animals on Earth. Allomothering is only one example of behavior that proves elephants are super smart.

Trunk Tools

An elephant's trunk is used to gather food, drink water, and bathe. But an elephant also uses its trunk as a tool. Researchers have seen elephants dig holes

Elephants use their trunks for eating, bathing, and playing.

with their trunks to find water. The elephants continue returning to the same spot for a drink. Elephants also grab tree branches with their trunks to swat flies away or to scratch themselves. An elephant's trunk is very agile. It can pick up a tiny coin from a flat surface. It can also lift an object weighing more than 550 pounds (250 kg). Elephants use their trunks in social ways. Many elephants use their trunks for hugging one another or playing.

Helping the Herd

Elephants learn many things on their own. They also teach one another. Elephants in eastern Africa taught other elephants how to tell local poachers apart from farmers. When elephants saw or

Elephant Mischief

Biologist George Wittemyer has found that some elephants use their trunks for mischief. In Africa, drinking water is often stored outside in large water tanks. People access the water by turning on a faucet. The elephants figured out how to lift the lids off human water tanks. The elephants drank all the water while the people slept. The thirsty elephants even figured out how to turn on water faucets.

Elephants living in the wild learn to tell hunters apart from farmers or other non-threatening people.

smelled the poachers, they ran away and took cover. Elephants that had never encountered the poachers before responded in the same way when they sensed the poachers nearby. Scientists think this is because the elephants were taught by example.

Elephant herds are close families that stick together. They understand when other herd members are in need. Scientists have seen elephants help fellow herd members. In one herd, a young female elephant broke her leg. The other elephants in her herd helped her with everyday tasks. Scientists believe the young elephant may not have survived without the help.

All About Personality

Researchers have identified four main personality types among elephant herds. In addition to a leader, each herd consists of happy females, playful elephants, and reliable family members. Other elephants respect the leader's intelligence and problem-solving skills. Happy females spend their time touching and rubbing against other herd members. Most young elephants are playful. A few elephants continue to be playful as adults. Elephants with reliable personalities care for calves. They remain calm even in unsafe situations.

Communication

Scientists listen to different elephant sounds with the help of technology. They have discovered elephants often communicate with each other. Common sounds include low growls and rumbles. Scientists believe elephants detect ground vibrations

When an elephant is excited, it lifts its trunk and makes a trumpet-like noise.

created from these sounds using sensors in their feet. Pregnant females make a special noise before giving birth. When herd members hear this, they look out for predators and form a circle to protect the new mother and her calf.

Elephants are known for making loud, trumpeting noises when they are excited. Each elephant sounds different. Scientists have found that a matriarch can

Elephants are able to remember where watering holes are within their home ranges.

recognize 100 different elephants by listening to the sounds they make.

Memory

Researchers have found that elephants have excellent memories. They recognize members of their herds even if they last saw each other decades ago. Research shows elephants recall the best places to migrate during droughts. Remembering this kind of information can save elephants' lives.

Science journalist Virginia Morell writes about animal intelligence tests in her book, *Animal Wise*. She writes about how researchers often learn new things while performing tests:

> In 2010, Kandula, a young male Asian elephant at the Smithsonian National Zoological Park in Washington, DC, was offered . . . [a] step stool. Kandula rolled the sturdy cube to the middle of his enclosure, stepped up on it, and snagged a suspended treat with his trunk . . . "The primary purpose of their trunks is to smell," said Preston Foerder, a graduate student at the City University of New York, who devised the successful elephant-insight test. So when an elephant is asked to hold a stick with its trunk to reach food, it can grasp the stick—but it can no longer locate the food. "It would be like having an eye in the palm of your hand, and then being asked to hold a tool and find food." Foerder said. "You wouldn't be able to do it."
>
> Source: Virginia Morell. *Animal Wise: The Thoughts and Emotions of Our Fellow Creatures. New York: Crown Publishers, 2013. Print. 137.*

Consider Your Audience

Read Morell's words closely. How would you adapt this excerpt for a different audience, such as your parents or younger friends? Write a blog post conveying this same information for the new audience. What is the best way to get the point across to your new audience?

CHAPTER FOUR

A PLACE TO CALL HOME

African elephants live south of the Sahara Desert in Africa. African bush elephants are a subspecies of the African elephant. They live in large grasslands called savannas. Another subspecies, the African forest elephant, lives in the tropical rain forests of western and central Africa.

Asian elephants live in South Asia and Southeast Asia. Asian elephants prefer to live near the edge

Elephants live in different African and Asian habitats.

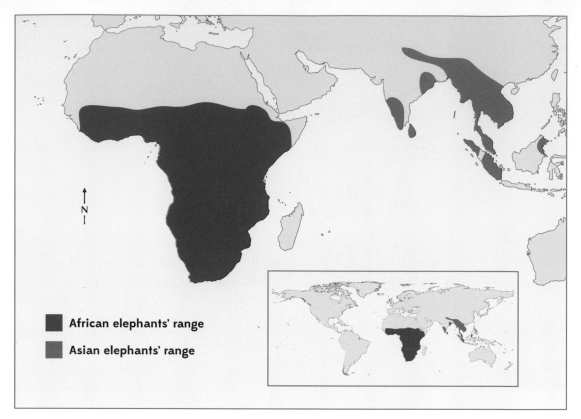

Elephants' Range

Look at the range map of the different locations African and Asian elephants call home. Why would elephants be well suited for life in these areas? Write a short paragraph describing the types of habitats in which elephants thrive.

of forests. These surroundings offer the low, woody plants they eat.

Elephant Diet

Elephants are herbivores. They eat different types of bark, fruit, grasses, leaves, and roots. Adult elephants

Elephants eat a lot of food to maintain their massive size, sometimes spending up to 16 hours a day eating or searching for food.

can eat 300 pounds (136 kg) of food each day. In order to find this much food, elephants travel great distances. Some elephants walk up to 25 miles (40 km) in one day.

Threats to Elephants

Like many other wild animals, elephants suffer from range loss. More people are moving into elephants' habitats. The Asian elephant lives in the most populated region of the world. It faces the greatest risk of extinction. It is currently listed as an endangered species. African elephants are listed as a vulnerable species, which means they could become endangered.

Because of their size, adult elephants have no natural predators. Lions or tigers occasionally eat young or weak elephants. Crocodiles have also been known to attack young elephants in the water. In most cases, young elephants are safe from predators when they remain with their herd.

An Elephant Tunnel

Some countries are finding creative ways to keep elephant herds safe in their home ranges. A major highway in Kenya once created an unsafe situation for elephants. The busy road separated the elephants from a large part of their range. Crossing the highway was the only way the elephants could reach the other side. It was unsafe for the elephants and the people driving. A 15-foot (5-m) tall tunnel was built under the

A tunnel was built in Kenya to keep elephants safe from humans and cars as the elephants moved around in their home range.

highway so the elephants could move to the other side without crossing the highway. Similar tunnels have been built in India.

Poachers

The biggest threat elephants face is poachers. Elephant hunting has been illegal in Africa and Asia since 1989. Poachers kill elephants illegally to sell their ivory tusks. Ivory is a prized material in many areas of the world. Demand for ivory is especially high in China. People will pay as much as $1,000 for a single pound of ivory.

Saving Elephants

Organizations such as the International Elephant Foundation and Save the Elephants work to protect elephants from range loss and poaching. Protection begins with research. By studying the elephants in their daily lives, researchers identify the best ways to protect their ranges. Conservation groups work with wildlife departments to prevent poachers from killing elephants for ivory.

FURTHER EVIDENCE

There is quite a bit of information about elephants' ranges in Chapter Four. It also covers threats to elephants. What do you think is the main point of the chapter? What evidence was given to support that point? Visit the Web site below to learn more about threats to Asian elephants. Choose a quote from the Web site that relates to this chapter. Does this quote support the author's main point? Does it make a new point? Write a few sentences explaining how the quote you found relates to this chapter.

Asian Elephant Threats
www.mycorelibrary.com/elephants

CHAPTER FIVE

DIFFERENT, YET MUCH THE SAME

Researchers have discovered many characteristics about elephants in the last several decades. In addition to using sounds to talk with one another, elephants use complex body language. Elephants appear to feel some of the same emotions people do. Scientists have gathered evidence that these enormous animals feel empathy for one another.

Scientists are beginning to understand more about elephants and their body language.

This means they can relate to what another elephant is feeling.

Elephant Emotions

Researchers have observed displays of empathy among elephants. In one case, an older elephant winced when she saw a younger elephant approach an electric fence. Researchers could tell by the older elephant's body language that it was worried the younger elephant was going to be hurt. The older elephant's posture and blinking eyes showed her worry.

Experts do not always agree about how animal emotions compare to human feelings. One of the

Researchers have witnessed elephants trying to stop younger elephants from getting hurt by dangerous objects, such as electric fences.

things that make elephants special is the way they deal with the death of another elephant. When a herd comes across the remains of an elephant, they stop to touch the body. Some researchers compare this

Elephant Body Language

Researchers have learned certain gestures mean different things among elephants. If an elephant folds its trunk under its tusks, it is probably asking another elephant to play. When elephants meet, they often rub shoulders. If an elephant stands upright, it is a sign for other animals to back off. When a group of elephants line up, they are probably ready to start a journey. You may even hear rumbles as they begin arguing about which direction to go.

act with humans taking a moment of silence to honor our dead.

Scientists are hopeful the future holds even more elephant discoveries. Some elephants are endangered and are threatened by certain human activities. It is important for humans to help take care of the areas elephants live in. Conserving these areas means scientists will continue to make amazing discoveries about elephants.

EXPLORE ONLINE

The focus in Chapter Five was on elephant research. It also touched on elephant emotions. The Web site below focuses on the same subjects. As you know, every source is different. How is the information given in the Web site different from the information in this chapter? What information is the same? How do the two sources present information differently? What can you learn from this Web site?

Elephant Emotions
www.mycorelibrary.com/elephants

FAST FACTS

Common Name: Elephant

Scientific Name: *Elephantidae*

Average Size: 9 to 12 feet (2.7 to 3.6 m) high at the shoulder (African elephant); 8 to 10.5 feet (2.4 to 3 m) high at the shoulder (Asian elephant)

Average Weight: Up to 15,000 pounds (6,803 kg) (African elephant); up to 12,000 pounds (5,500 kg) (Asian elephant)

Color: Varying shades of gray and brown

Lifespan: Up to 70 years in the wild; shorter lifespan when living in captivity

Diet: Plants, bark, grass, leaves, and fruit

Habitat: Africa, in many areas south of the Sahara Desert; elephants also live in several South and Southeast Asian countries

Threats: Humans

Intelligence Features

- Elephants use their trunks for many purposes, including eating, bathing, and exploring their surroundings.
- Elephants teach one another things they have learned.
- Elephants make a variety of sounds to communicate with one another.
- Elephants have good memories. They remember other elephants even if they have not seen them for many years.

STOP AND THINK

Say What?

Learning about elephants can mean learning a lot of new vocabulary. Find five words in this book that you've never heard or seen before. Use a dictionary to find out what they mean. Using your own ideas, write down the meaning of each word. Then use each word in a new sentence.

Another View

There are many different sources about elephants. As you know, every source is different. Ask a librarian or another adult to help you find a reliable source about elephants. Write a short essay comparing and contrasting the new source's point of view to the ideas in this book. How are the sources similar or different? Why do you think they are similar or different?

Why Do I Care?

This book discusses how human activity has caused elephant populations to decline. Why should this concern you? Write down two or three reasons humans should care about decline in elephant populations.

Surprise Me

Learning about elephants can be interesting and surprising. Think about what you learned. Can you name two or three facts about elephants you found surprising? Write a short paragraph about each fact. Why did you find them surprising?

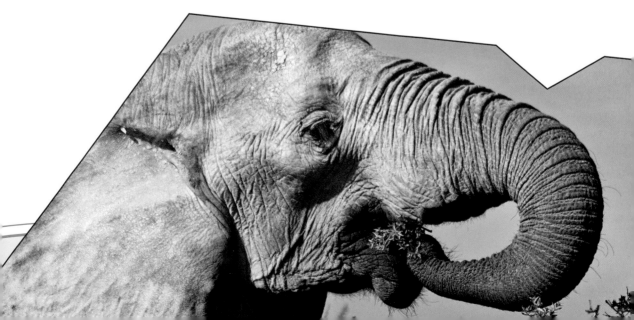

GLOSSARY

agile
able to move quickly and
easily

captive
kept within bounds

empathy
identification with the
feelings of another

herbivore
an animal that survives by
eating plant material

matriarch
the female head of a family

placid
pleasantly calm or peaceful

poacher
a person who hunts animals
illegally

predator
an animal that survives by
hunting and eating other
animals

subspecies
a category of animals that
ranks below the species
category

volatile
threatening to become
violent

zoologist
a scientist who studies
animals

LEARN MORE

Books

Allen, Thomas B. *Animals of Africa*. New York: Rizzoli Publications, 2008.

Joubert, Beverly, and Dereck Joubert. *Face to Face with Elephants*. Washington, DC: National Geographic Children's Books, 2008.

Pelusy, Michael, and Jane Pelusy. *Elephants*. Tarrytown, NY: Marshall Cavendish, 2009.

Web Links

To learn more about elephants, visit ABDO Publishing Company online at **www.abdopublishing.com**. Web sites about elephants are featured on our Book Links page. These links are routinely monitored and updated to provide the most current information available.

Visit **www.mycorelibrary.com** for free additional tools for teachers and students.

INDEX

ABOUT THE AUTHOR

Tammy Gagne has written dozens of books for both adults and children. She resides in northern New England with her husband, son, and pets. One of her favorite pastimes is visiting schools to speak to children about the writing process.